FAMOUS florida!

Orange Recipes

Famous Recipes From Famous Places

FAMOUS florida!

y Joyce LaFray

Manufactured in the United States of America

International Standard Book Number: 0-942084-69-1
Library of Congress Card Catalog Number: 87-051518

For additional copies, write directly to:

Seaside
Publishing, Inc.
P.O. Box 14441
St. Petersburg, Florida 33733-4441

01 02 03 04 05- ML-00 99

TABLE OF CONTENTS

Take a little bit of Florida sunshine, a few drops of crystal clear rain, a handful of rich, organic soil, and a plump little white seed and you can grow the sweetest, juiciest, most delicious orange in the world.

Florida Oranges: The Origins

Oranges always were thought to be an exotic fruit. The Renaissance painters thought that the orange originated in Palestine and often included orange trees in their paintings. European royalty coveted the sweet and colorful fruit. In fact, French monarch Louis XIV built special indoor groves in which he held lavish garden parties and balls. One of these buildings appropriately named the "Orangerie" still exists in Paris, and houses paintings of the Impressionists. The common man also considered the orange a real treat. Oranges were sold in theatres, gift boxes and by street vendors.

There are two types of oranges commonly eaten and grown in the United States today: the sweet orange, which is referred to in ancient Chinese manuscripts dating back as far as 2200 B.C.; and the bitter, Seville orange, which originally came from India. These luscious fruits traveled aboard many seaworthy vessels to all parts of the world.

The orange had its beginning in the United States when Christopher Columbus and Spanish conquistadores brought the first oranges to Florida. The Spaniards planted citrus trees wherever they settled, and Indians dropped seeds throughout the state, much like "Johnny Appleseed" once spread his apple seeds.

In the early 1800's, most orange groves were located around St. Augustine, Tampa Bay and along the St. Johns River. But severe winter weather caused the groves to move to warmer locations along the coastlines. By the 1900's, the northeastern part of the state ceased being a major citrus producing area, for the groves had relocated to central Florida where the trees were not subjected to freezing conditions.

The Orange Tree

Central Florida's citrus belt looks like a game of dot-to-dot which runs for thousands of square miles. Trees are planted in straight rows, making graphic patterns on the rich soil.

Since ancient times, the orange tree has been a symbol of beauty and its blossom, a symbol of love. A mature orange tree can grow up to about 30 feet and has symmetrical branches with dark green leaves that last year round. Its flowers are white and wax-like. It smells divine, and frequently is used to make orange blossom honey and perfume.

The Fruit

The role of diet in health is becoming an increasingly important issue in today's world. Not only do people want to slim down; they also want to be fit.

Oranges, a perfect nutritional choice, add a variety of essential nutrients to your diet, principally ascorbic acid (Vitamin C), potassium, Folic acid, thiamine (Vitamin B1) and other B vitamins. They add bulk to the diet and are helpful in lowering serum cholesterol. Each orange contains only about 100 calories and its natural sugar digests easily, giving one a quick energy boost.

Florida's Gift

Oranges are undoubtedly one of Florida's greatest gifts. Because Florida is the leading producer of oranges in the nation, it supplies superior quality fruit, juice concentrate, and juice in crystalized form to most of the United States year round.

In addition to wonderful marmalades, syrups, ice creams, and candied and jellied products, oranges are used in the production of such non-food items as perfume, alcohol, cosmetics, textiles, paints and insecticides.

How to Store

To keep a Florida orange fresh and to retain its vitamins, you must store it in the refrigerator at 35^0 to 50^0 F. Plastic bags and wrap should not be used, as they retain moisture and promote the growth of mold.

Carefully pick oranges that have not been damaged in shipping; then wash, dry and place them in a dry spot in your refrigerator.

Peel and Section

Oranges are easily used in cooking and baking when peeled and cut into individual sections. Take care to remove the pith and pulp. Here's how to peel:

First, using a stainless steel utility knife, cut slices from both ends of the orange. **Next**, cut off the peel from top to bottom, removing any remaining membrane. **Then**, with a slanted blade, slice along the membrane to the center, dividing the orange into sections. **Continue** to slice around the orange until all the segments are ready to use.

Orange Cookery

Oranges will whet your appetite, and that of your family and friends. From soups and salads, to breads, relishes and entrees, oranges enrich, garnish and add a zesty flavor to a meal. They are a gourmet's delight when added to seafood casseroles, fancy sauces, tropical beverages or hearty citrus chicken. Whether carried to work in a brown bag, or cooked in a delicate souffle, oranges are a perfect accompaniment to any meal.

I guarantee when you try some of the recipes in this cookbook, you'll fall in love with the Florida orange, too!

ORANGE PICKLED HERRING

2	12-ounce jars of herring in wine sauce
2	cups sugar
1/2	cup white wine vinegar
1	6-ounce can frozen Florida orange juice, undiluted
2	bay leaves
4	peppercorns
2	oranges
2	onions, thinly sliced

Drain herring and set aside. Mix sugar and vinegar in a bowl; add undiluted frozen orange juice, bay leaves and peppercorns. Pare oranges, cut peel into thin strips. Add peel to marinade. (Save orange pulp for another recipe). Add herring and onions and mix. Refrigerate overnight. Serve with rye crackers or thinly sliced pumpernickel.

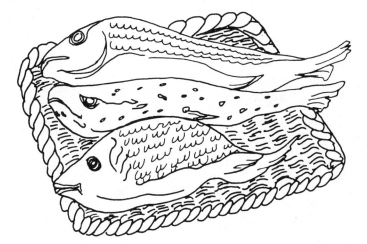

Serves: 6

ORANGE CONSOMME

1	quart chicken bouillon
2	envelopes plain gelatin
2	egg whites, lightly beaten
1/4	teaspoon ground ginger
1/8	teaspoon nutmeg
	Salt and finely ground white pepper to taste
3	cups fresh Florida orange juice, strained
1	unpeeled Florida orange, cut crosswise into very thin slices

Skim all fat from the chicken bouillon and pour into a saucepan. Sprinkle gelatin on the bouillon and let stand for 3-4 minutes. Add the egg whites and, stirring constantly, bring to boil over high heat. Cook for 2-3 minutes, remove from heat and let cool for 10 minutes. Add ginger, nutmeg, salt and pepper. Line a fine sieve with cheesecloth and strain the mixture through the cloth letting it drip slowly. Add orange juice and refrigerate overnight. Serve in chilled cups, garnished with orange slices.

Serves: 6

SUNNY DAY SOUP

6	whole fresh Florida oranges
2	bananas
1	small can (8-1/2 ounces) crushed pineapple
1	small jar maraschino cherries
1/2	cup sugar
2	ounces grated coconut

Peel, seed and section Florida oranges. Put in blender. Blend, then pour into bowl. Next, place bananas, pineapple with juice, and cherries in blender. Blend and mix well with oranges. Add sugar and stir into mixture. Pour into soup dishes and sprinkle with coconut. Serve chilled.

Serves: 6

JUDY'S DELIGHT

3	Florida oranges, sectioned
3	Florida grapefruits, sectioned
2	cucumbers, sliced
2	onions, sliced
1	apple, cored and cubed
1	cup Florida orange juice
1	cup wine vinegar
3/4	cup sugar
1 1/2	teaspoons salt
1/4	teaspoon pepper

In medium bowl combine orange sections, grapefruit sections, cucumbers, onions and apple. In a small bowl beat together orange juice, vinegar, sugar, salt and pepper. Pour over fruit and vegetables. Cover and chill for 1 1/2 - 3 hours. Serve on lettuce leaves. This marinade can also be used for marinating poultry or ham.

Serves: 4-6

ORANGE AND ONION SALAD

3	Florida oranges
2	large mild onions, thinly sliced
	Juice of 1 lime
1/2	cup Florida orange juice
2	teaspoons minced basil
4	tablespoons olive oil
	Salt and pepper to taste
	A few grains of cayenne pepper
6	sprigs watercress

Peel the oranges and remove all pith. Discard the seeds and coarsely chop the orange sections. In a bowl, toss orange pieces and onion together. Refrigerate for 1 hour. In a separate small bowl, whisk together lime and orange juice, basil, olive oil, salt, pepper and cayenne pepper.

Place the orange and onion mixture on to 6 chilled salad plates. Pour the lime-orange dressing over the oranges and onions. Garnish with a sprig of watercress.

Serves: 6

ORANGE AND CELERY SALAD

6	Florida oranges
3/4	cup chopped celery
1/4	cup French dressing
	Chopped mint
	Salad greens

Section the oranges and combine with celery and dressing. Let marinate at least 2 hours. Arrange mixture on salad greens and sprinkle with mint.

Serves: 6

SWEET POTATOES IN ORANGES

6	sweet potatoes
6	large Florida oranges
6	tablespoons heavy cream
3	tablespoons butter
1/3	cup sugar
	Salt to taste
1/4	teaspoon nutmeg
1/4	teaspoon cinnamon
	Peel from orange tops, sliced into thin strips

Boil the sweet potatoes for 30 minutes until tender. Drain the potatoes, peel and mash in a bowl. Slice the tops off 5 oranges and scoop out the flesh without breaking the shells. Squeeze the juice from the pulp and place in separate bowl. Add together cream, butter, sugar, salt, nutmeg, and cinnamon. Blend until smooth. Grate the rind of the sixth orange, add to the potato mixture and add 1/4 cup of the squeezed orange juice. Mix until well blended. Pipe the potato mixture into the orange shells through a pastry bag, affixed with a #6 tip, or spoon into the orange shells.

Place oranges into a baking dish and bake in a 350°F. oven for 25-30 minutes or until delicately browned. Serve garnished with the orange strips.

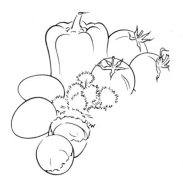

Serves: 6

GOLDEN YAMS

8	yams or sweet potatoes
1/3	cup margarine
3	tablespoons honey
1/2	teaspoon nutmeg
1/4	teaspoon cinnamon
1/4	teaspoon ginger
4	Florida oranges, sectioned

Scrub and dry unpared yams. Bake on oven rack or on baking sheet in 350⁰ F. oven for 45-60 minutes, until tender when tested with fork. When potatoes are almost done, melt margarine in saucepan; stir in honey and spices; heat until bubbly. Add orange sections and gently heat through. Split potatoes lengthwise, cutting almost but not all the way through; top with warm citrus sections.

Serves: 8

BROCCOLI WITH FRESH ORANGE SAUCE

1	bunch fresh broccoli
2	tablespoons margarine
2	tablespoons flour
1/2	cup Florida orange juice
1/2	cup plain yogurt
1/2	teaspoon salt
1/2	teaspoon grated orange rind
1/4	dried leaf thyme

Wash broccoli and remove large leaves and tough part of stalks. Cut into individual spears. Place in large saucepan with 1/2-inch boiling water. Cover; simmer 10-12 minutes, until broccoli is crisp and tender.

Meanwhile, melt margarine in small saucepan. Remove from heat; blend in flour until smooth. Gradually stir in remaining ingredients; cook over low heat, stirring constantly, until mixture thickens. Drain broccoli well. Serve with orange sauce.

Serves: 4

ORANGE GLAZED BARBECUED SPARERIBS

4	3-pound racks of ribs

Sauce

	Juice of 2 lemons
	Juice of 6 large Florida oranges
	Peel of 2 large Florida oranges, grated
1	quart ketchup
1/2	cup cider vinegar
1/2	cup Dijon mustard
2	cups brown sugar
1	cup Worcestershire sauce
2	cloves garlic, finely minced
1	tablespoon celery salt
	Freshly ground pepper to taste
1	teaspoon cayenne pepper
	Dill pickle juice (optional)

Add together the lemon and orange juice. Stir in the orange peel. Add the ketchup, cider vinegar, mustard brown sugar, and Worcestershire sauce. Mix well. Season with the garlic, celery salt, and black and cayenne peppers. If necessary, thin the sauce with dill pickle juice.

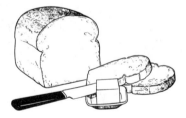

Serves: 6

ORANGE LAMB ROLL

2 1/2	pounds boneless lamb, butterflied and flattened
4	tablespoons sunflower oil
1	teaspoon ground orange rind
3	cloves garlic, mashed
3	teaspoons peeled ginger root, minced
1	cup coarsely grated carrot
1	red bell pepper, diced
6	scallions, chopped
	Salt and pepper to taste
1	orange with peel cut into thin strips
4	red dry chili peppers
2 1/2	tablespoons light brown sugar
1 1/2	cups beef broth
2	cups Florida orange juice
3	tablespoons soy sauce
3	temple oranges, peeled with all pith removed, sliced thin crosswise
	Minced parsley for garnish

Preheat oven to 350⁰ F. Pound the lamb to about 3/4-inch thickness. In a skillet heat 2 tablespoons oil; add ground orange rind, garlic, and 1 teaspoon ginger root. Stir and saute for 2 minutes. Add the grated carrot, mix well and cook for 1 minute longer. Add the red bell pepper and scallions. Salt and pepper to taste. Toss lightly. Sprinkle lamb with salt and pepper. Spread the carrot mixture over the lamb. Roll the lamb into a tight cylinder and tie the roll with kitchen string at 2-inch intervals.

Use a dutch oven or a large oven-proof kettle and heat the remaining oil. Add the orange peel and the chili peppers and cook for 1-2 minutes. Remove orange peel and chili peppers from the kettle onto a plate and set aside. Add the lamb roll to the kettle, sprinkle with brown sugar, spreading evenly over the roll. Add beef broth, orange juice, remaining garlic, remaining ginger root, soy sauce

(continued)

ORANGE LAMB ROLL continued

and the sauteed orange peel and chili peppers. Bring the liquid to boil and simmer roll, turning occasionally for 10 minutes. Place kettle into preheated oven and bake for 1 to 2 hours or until the meat feels tender when pierced with a fork.

Remove roll from kettle and place on a cutting board. Strain the cooking juices into a saucepan, and cook until reduced by about half. Poach orange slices in the liquid for 2 minutes. Remove string from lamb roll and slice the roll into 1-inch slices. Place on a heated platter. Garnish with poached orange slices, pour sauce over the lamb slices and sprinkle with parsley.

Serves: 6

ORANGY PORK CHOPS

3	tablespoons butter
6	8-ounce center cut pork chops, well trimmed
	Salt and pepper to taste
1 1/2	cups Florida orange juice
1/2	cup dark brown sugar
	Juice of 1 lemon
2	tablespoons ground ginger
	Grated rind of 1 orange
6	Florida orange slices, cut very thin and seeded

Preheat oven to 375⁰ F. Heat butter in a large skillet and brown the chops on both sides. Sprinkle with salt and pepper. Place the chops in a single layer into a baking dish. Discard the butter. In a bowl, blend orange juice, brown sugar, lemon juice, ginger and grated orange rind and pour over the chops. Place orange slices on the chops. Bake chops in the oven for 35-40 minutes until they are tender. Baste frequently with the pan juices. Place chops on a heated platter. Strain pan juices, adjust seasoning and cook in a small saucepan until thickened and pour over the chops. Serve immediately.

Serves: 6

SPICED BEEF a L'ORANGE

3	tablespoons butter
3	pounds sirloin of beef cut into l-inch cubes
	Salt and pepper to taste
3/4	cup dry white wine
1 1/3	cups orange juice
2	tablespoons cornstarch
	Grated rind of 1 Florida orange
1/3	cup golden raisins
2	cloves garlic, minced
1	teaspoon chili powder
1/8	teaspoon ground cloves
1/4	teaspoon nutmeg
2	Florida oranges, peeled, divided, with seeds and pits removed

Preheat oven to 350⁰ F. In a large skillet, heat butter until it begins to brown. Add beef cubes and turn the meat quickly to brown on all sides. With a slotted spoon, remove the meat and place in a baking dish or casserole and sprinkle with salt and pepper. Pour wine and 1 cup of orange juice into the skillet where meat was browned. Bring to boil and simmer until reduced by about 1/4. Mix cornstarch with remaining 1/3 cup orange juice, add to the skillet. Stir well and cook on high heat for 1-2 minutes, stirring constantly until smooth and slightly thickened. Stir in the grated orange rind, raisins, garlic, chili powder, cloves and nutmeg. Bring to boil once and pour over the meat in the casserole. Stir the meat to coat with the orange mixture.

Bake the beef in a preheated oven for 1 1/2 hours. Add the orange sections and bake for 15 minutes longer. Serve over white rice, sprinkled with minced parsley. May be cooled, refrigerated and reheated next day.

Serves: 6

ORANGE CHICKEN WITH RAISINS AND ALMONDS

1	frying chicken, cut into small pieces
1	cup flour
1	teaspoon salt
1/2	teaspoon black pepper
1/2	teaspoon crushed fennel seed
1/4	cup melted butter
1 1/2	cups Florida orange juice
1	teaspoon orange rind, finely grated
2/3	cup crushed pineapple, well drained
1/4	cup sugar
1/4	teaspoon ginger
1/4	teaspoon cinnamon
2/3	cup raisins
1	cup pale dry Sherry wine
1/2	cup coarsely chopped blanched almonds

Preheat oven to 350⁰F. Pat the chicken dry with a paper towel. Mix flour, salt, pepper, and crushed fennel seed. Dredge chicken in flour mixture. Pour butter into a skillet and brown the chicken on both sides. Place the chicken into a well buttered baking dish or casserole. In a bowl, combine orange juice, rind, pineapple, sugar, ginger, cinnamon, raisins and the Sherry. Pour into the skillet where the chicken was cooking. Season with salt and pepper to taste. Bring to a boil and pour over the chicken. Bake in a preheated oven for 35-40 minutes. Sprinkle with almonds and serve immediately.

Serves: 4

CREPES SPIRITUELLE

Crepes

8	eggs
2	cups light cream
1 1/2	cups club soda
5	tablespoons melted butter
1/2	teaspoon salt
2	tablespoons sugar
2	cups all purpose flour, sifted
1/2	cup clarified butter* (recipe follows)
	Orange Sauce (recipe follows)

In a blender, combine eggs and cream and mix for a few seconds. Add club soda, butter, salt, sugar and flour. Blend until very smooth. Scrape down sides of the blender and mix again for a few seconds until very smooth. Let stand 1 hour covered.

Heat a 5-inch crepe pan and brush it with clarified butter. Pour in a little of the batter and tip the pan immediately so it spreads evenly over the entire surface. Cook crepes quickly on both sides. Repeat until all the crepes are cooked. Stack the crepes on a warm plate. Cover with wax paper to prevent drying out if crepes are to be filled later.

Crepes may be refrigerated for up to 3 days. They may also be frozen. To freeze: place wax paper between crepes and wrap in foil. To use: defrost overnight in the refrigerator or place crepes wrapped in foil in a 200⁰ F. oven for about 25-30 minutes. Remove and separate carefully. If not completely defrosted, rewrap and return to the oven. Use crepes immediately.

*Clarified Butter – In a saucepan, melt butter or margarine. Let cool for about 1/2 hour. Then remove white sediment from top, pour off golden liquid and discard white sediment from bottom. The clarified butter should be stored in a jar with a tight lid in the refrigerator. It will keep for about 2 months.

CREPES *continued*

ORANGE SAUCE

1/4	pound unsalted butter
1	cup sugar, or more to taste
	Grated rind of 1 orange
	Grated rind of 1 lemon
6	tablespoons frozen concentrated Florida orange juice*
1/2	cup Florida orange juice
1/2	teaspoon cinnamon
1/3	cup Cointreau, or any orange liqueur
1/4	cup orange liqueur or brandy for flambe
1	cup confectioners' sugar

In a large skillet, combine butter and sugar and cook until butter is melted. Add the orange and lemon rinds and cook, stirring until mixture thickens. Add the frozen concentrated orange juice, fresh orange juice and cinnamon. Cook on low heat until thickened. Add the Cointreau or any orange liqueur. Place the crepes into the sauce and fold into quarters. Simmer for a few minutes.

In a small pan heat brandy or liqueur until just lukewarm. Do not overheat. Ignite and pour over the crepes. When flames die down, serve crepes sprinkled with confectioners' sugar.

*Do not defrost. This recipe may also be used for dessert, of course!

Yield: 24 small crepes

FLOUNDER WITH ORANGE SAUCE

6	8-ounce fresh flounder fillets
1	tablespoon butter, melted
3	cloves garlic, mashed
1	tablespoon grated orange rind
1/4	teaspoon white pepper
	Florida orange sections
	Parsley sprigs

Preheat oven to 400⁰ F. Butter a baking dish with 1 tablespoon butter. Place fillets in baking dish. Combine garlic, orange rind and white pepper, and pour over the fish. Cover the baking dish with foil and place into oven. Bake for 20-25 minutes or until fish flakes easily. While the fish is baking, prepare sauce.

Orange Sauce

4	tablespoons butter
3	cloves garlic, sliced
2	tablespoons parsley, minced
	Juice of 1 orange
1/8	teaspoon nutmeg
1/8	teaspoon ginger
1	teaspoon dry mustard
	Salt and pepper to taste

In a saucepan, heat the butter, add the garlic and cook until the garlic begins to brown. With a slotted spoon, remove garlic and discard. Add parsley, orange juice, nutmeg, ginger, mustard, salt and pepper to taste. Bring to a boil and cook until slightly thickened. Pour over the fish. Garnish with orange sections and sprigs of parsley. Serve immediately.

Serves: 6

ROAST CRISP DUCKLING L'ORANGE

(Allow 24 hours to prepare ahead)

1	4-5 pound duckling
	Salt and papper to taste
1	teaspoon oregano
1/2	orange

SAUCE

1	6-ounce can frozen Florida orange juice concentrate
1	cup apricots with juice, peeled and pitted
1/4	cup dark brown sugar
2	tablespoons lemon juice
1	tablespoon Triple Sec
1	tablespoon brandy

Preheat oven to 350⁰ F. Sprinkle duck with salt, pepper and rub oregano over all. Insert the orange half into cavity. Roast for about 2 hours or until tender. Cool. Wrap in foil and refrigerate until next day.

Prepare sauce by blending ingredients in the container of a food processor or a blender. Roast the duck for 1/2 hour after basting with sauce. Continue to baste with the orange sauce until duck is hot and covered entirely with sauce.

Serves: 2-3

GLAZED VEAL MEDALLIONS

3	tablespoons butter
12	3-ounce slices veal tenderloin
2/3	cup Florida orange juice
1/3	cup orange liqueur
1/4	teaspoon ground nutmeg
1/4	teaspoon ground allspice
	Salt and pepper to taste
12	artichoke bottoms, cooked
24	orange sections with pith removed
	Orange Aspic (recipe follows)

In large skillet, melt butter; saute veal lightly on both sides until golden. Remove from skillet and place in shallow pan. Add orange juice to skillet; simmer until reduced by half. Add orange liqueur, nutmeg, allspice, salt and pepper to taste. Bring to a boil; pour over medallions. Cool. Cover. Refrigerate. Serve chilled veal medallions on artichoke bottoms, garnished with orange sections. Glaze veal with Orange Aspic (recipe follows). Chill before serving.

Orange Aspic

2	tablespoons unflavored gelatin
1	cup chicken broth
3/4	cup Florida orange juice

In sauce pan, sprinkle gelatin over chicken broth; let stand 1 minute. Add orange juice and mix well. Stir over low heat until gelatin dissolves. Remove from heat. Cool and glaze tenderloins.

Refrigerate the remaining aspic. When aspic has set, dice the aspic and sprinkle around the veal medallions for garnish.

Serves: 6

ORANGE HORSERADISH SAUCE

2   tablespoons Florida juice concentrate, undiluted
1   cup plain yogurt
1-2   tablespoons coarse white horseradish (more or less to taste)
             Cayenne pepper to taste
2   tablespoons honey or more to taste

Blend all the ingredients together until smooth. Add more horseradish or pepper and honey to taste.

Yield: 1 1/2 cups

ORANGE CHUTNEY

6	Florida oranges
4	cups water
2	cups finely chopped onions
2	cups dark brown sugar
1	cup chopped pitted prunes
1	cup raisins
1/2	cup dark rum
1 1/2	teaspoons salt and more if necessary
1/2	teaspoon crushed coriander
1/4	teaspoon nutmeg
1/8	teaspoon black pepper
1/2	cup wine vinegar or more to taste

Peel oranges and cut the peel into very thin strips. Cook oranges or peel in 2 cups water for about 5 minutes. Drain. Cook 5 minutes again in 2 cups fresh water. Drain. Remove membrane and pits from oranges and chop them up. Combine oranges, onions, dark brown sugar, prunes and orange peel. Cook on medium heat covered for about 30 minutes, or until thickened.

Soak raisins in the rum for 10 minutes. Add raisins, salt, coriander, nutmeg, black pepper and vinegar. Cook 10-15 minutes longer until very thick. Cool and fill into sterilized jars according to manufacturer's directions. Store in a cool dry place or refrigerator.

Note: According to your taste you may want to add more sugar, salt, vinegar or pepper.

Serves: 10

SOUFFLE A L'ORANGE

	Grated rind of 1 Florida orange (about 3 tablespoons)
3	tablespoons butter
3	tablespoons flour
1 1/2	cups milk
	Pinch of salt
6	egg yolks
2/3	cup sugar
1/4	cup Cointreau orange liqueur
2	tablespoons orange extract or flavoring
7	egg whites
1/8	teaspoon cream of tartar powder
	Grated Florida orange rind and 1/4 cup sugar for garnish

Preheat oven to 350⁰ F. Butter well and sprinkle with sugar a 2-quart souffle dish. Grate the rind of one orange. In a saucepan melt butter, add the flour, stir it with wooden spoon. Be sure not to let it brown. Add lukewarm (never hot) milk stirring constantly to avoid lumps. Cook for about 3 minutes on low heat until the sauce thickens. Remove from heat. Add salt and all the egg yolks at once, beating steadily with wire whisk or spoon to avoid curdling. Beat until yolks are well absorbed. Add orange rind, sugar, Cointreau and orange flavoring.

Beat the whites with cream of tartar until stiff. Fold into the orange mixture, very gently. Pour into the souffle dish. Place souffle dish into the oven and bake for 40-45 minutes, or until inserted knife comes out clean.

Have some grated orange rind and 1/4 cup granulated sugar at hand. As soon as the souffle is ready, sprinkle with rind and sugar. Serve immediately.

Serves: 4-6

CREPES AMBROSIA

2	cups Florida orange sections, halved
1	cup Florida grapefruit sections, cut into pieces
2	cups heavy cream
1/4	sugar
2	teaspoons grated orange rind
1	cup flaked coconut
1	cup maraschino cherries, drained and quartered

Drain orange and grapefruit pieces on paper towels. Combine heavy cream and sugar; beat until stiff. Fold in grated rind, orange and grapefruit pieces, coconut and cherries.

To fill crepe, fold into cone shape or cornucopia and fill with citrus-cream mixture or spread crepe with cream mixture and roll.

Yield: Filling for 24 crepes

FLORIDA AMBROSIA

3	Florida grapefruit
3	Florida oranges
1	cup fresh strawberries, sliced
3	tablespoons sugar
1/4	cup flaked coconut

Section all grapefruit and 2 oranges. Slice remaining peeled orange crosswise, 1/4 inch thick. Combine grapefruit, oranges and strawberries. Sprinkle with sugar if desired. Turn into serving bowl and sprinkle with coconut.

Serves: 8

ORANGE CHOCOLATE CRUNCH

2	cups fresh Florida orange sections (6 oranges)
1/2	cup Florida orange juice
2	eggs
1	teaspoon vanilla extract
1/4	teaspoon almond extract
1 2/3	cups flour
1	cup sugar
1	teaspoon baking powder
1/2	teaspoon baking soda
1/2	teaspoon salt
1/2	cup light brown sugar
1	cup chopped walnuts
6	ounces semi-sweet chocolate bits

Preheat oven to 350⁰ F. Peel and section Florida oranges. Cut sections into small pieces. Combine orange pieces and orange juice. Beat eggs and add oranges and juice mixture, vanilla and almond extracts. Mix well. Sift dry ingredients and add all at once. Pour into a greased and floured 13" x 9" x 2" inch baking pan.

Combine brown sugar, nuts and chocolate bits. Sprinkle on top of cake. Bake for 45-50 minutes.

Serves: 20

CHOCOLATE ORANGE AND CINNAMON ICE CREAM

Zest	of 3 Florida oranges
4	cups heavy cream
4	sticks cinnamon
8	ounces semi-sweet chocolate
8	egg yolks
1	cup sugar
1	teaspoon vanilla extract

Remove the zest from 3 oranges with a potato peeler. Put the orange zest in a saucepan with the cream and cinnamon sticks. Bring the cream up to a boil, then remove the pan from the heat. Cover the pan and allow the cream to steep for two hours.

Put the chocolate in a small pan and melt over low heat. Stir continually until the chocolate is "scorched" and thick. Put the chocolate in a large bowl or container. Set aside.

Beat the yolks with 1/4 cup of sugar until they are well combined. Strain the cinnamon and orange peel from the cream. Bring the cream and the remaining 3/4 cup of sugar up to a boil. Add a bit of the hot cream to the egg yolks and then add the yolks back into the cream, stirring constantly. Over medium heat, stir the mixture until it is thick but DO NOT BOIL. Strain this mixture into the scorched chocolate and stir until thoroughly combined. Allow the mixture to cool completely. Freeze in an ice cream machine according to the manufacturer's instructions.

Serves: 4-6

From the QUADY WINERY, Madeira, California

BEST ORANGE MOUSSE

	Vegetable oil
9	egg yolks
1 1/2	cups granulated sugar
1	tablespoon finely grated orange rind
1	tablespoon orange extract flavoring
1	cup orange juice
2	packages unflavored gelatin
2/3	cup orange liqueur
3 1/2	cups heavy whipping cream
1/2	cup powdered sugar
9	egg whites
1	Florida orange, unpeeled and thinly sliced

Oil a 1 1/2-quart souffle dish and sprinkle with sugar. Tie a well-oiled waxed paper collar around the dish, extending 6" above the dish. Wrap collar snugly around the dish and attach with scotch tape so it holds together securely.

In a large bowl, beat together egg yolks and granulated sugar until thick and lemon colored. Add orange rind and flavoring. Heat orange juice but do not boil. Dissolve gelatin in the orange liqueur and mix into hot orange juice. Slowly pour orange juice mixture into egg yolk mixture, beating constantly; cool.

Now, whip the cream until slightly thickened, add powdered sugar and whip until stiff. Reserve 1 cup of this whipped cream for decoration. Fold remaining whipped cream into egg yolk mixture.

Whip egg whites until stiff but not dry. Fold into yolk mixture thoroughly but gently. Pour mousse into prepared souffle dish very carefully. Do not bend or disturb the paper collar. Refrigerate for at least 4- 5 hours overnight. Before serving remove paper collar. Leave mousse in souffle dish -do not unmold. Top with remaining whipped cream and orange slices.

Serves: 8-10

STEAMED ORANGE BREAD PUDDING

6	slices stale white bread
1 1/2	cups scalded milk
1	cup Florida orange juice
1	tablespoon orange rind
4	eggs, beaten
2/3	cup sugar
1/8	teaspoon salt
1/3	cup orange marmalade
1/2	teaspoon vanilla extract
1/2	cup raisins (optional)
	Sweetened whipped cream or fruit syrup

Preheat oven to 375⁰ F. Butter well a 1 1/2-quart steamed pudding mold or any deep baking dish. Sprinkle generously with granulated sugar.

Cut crust off bread. Slice bread into small cubes. Scald milk, add bread cubes and soak for 10 minutes. Add orange juice and rind. Beat eggs with sugar and salt until thick and lemon colored. Add to bread and milk. Fold in orange marmalade, vanilla and, if desired, raisins. Pour bread mixture into buttered mold. Place mold into a basting pan and pour hot water into the pan. Bake pudding for 55 minutes, or until tip of knife inserted into pudding comes out clean. Cook for 10-15 minutes.

Loosen around edges with a knife. Invert onto a p:atter and unmold. Serve hot or cold with whipped cream or a fruit syrup. NOTE: If you double this recipe, increase baking time to 1 1/2 hours. Test for doneness with a knife.

Serves: 6

PERFECT ORANGE FLAN

Glaze

1/2	cup sugar
2	tablespoons orange marmalade
1	tablespoon Florida orange juice
1 1/2	quart charlotte mold or a steamed pudding mold

Flan

3	cups heavy cream, scalded
6	eggs
2/3	cup granulated sugar
1	teaspoon Florida orange extract
1	tablespoon grated orange rind
1	Florida orange, thinly sliced for garnishing

In a small saucepan blend together sugar, marmalade and juice. Cook over low heat until sugar is completely melted, stirring occasionally. Drip a few drips on to a cold plate and see if the mixture hardens. If it is still liquid, cook a little longer, testing frequently. When ready, pour the glaze into the mold and turn and tilt the mold to coat with the glaze. If you wish, use a pastry brush to spread the glaze. The mold should be evenly coated. Put mold into the refrigerator until the glaze is completely set.

Preheat oven to 350⁰ F. Scald the cream. Beat the eggs with the sugar, add the extract and rind. Pour in the hot cream and beat a few second more. Pour into the glazed charlotte mold. Set mold into a pan of hot water and bake in oven for 50 minutes or until a knife inserted into the flan comes out clean. Cool completely. Refrigerate for about 3 hours.

Unmold onto a platter. There will be liquid in the mold which will run down sides of flan and pieces of orange from the marmalade on top of flan, which makes it very decorative. Garnish the flan with thinly sliced oranges dipped into the glaze.

Serves: 4

FLORIDA FRESH ORANGE PIE

Orange Flavoring

2	large Florida oranges
4	lumps sugar
1	cup fresh Florida orange juice
1 1/2	tablespoons gelatin
5	egg whites
1/4	teaspoon salt
1	tablespoon granulated sugar

Custard Sauce

7	egg yolks
1	cup granulated sugar
2	teaspoons cornstarch
1 1/2	cups boiling milk
3/4	cup cold whipping cream

Wash oranges and rub lump sugar over them until sugar is impregnated with orange oil. Mash sugar lumps in mixing bowl and grate orange skins in bowl. Sprinkle gelatin over one cup fresh Florida orange juice. Add 7 egg yolks to mixing bowl containing sugar until mixture forms ribbons. Then beat in cornstarch (2 minutes). Beat boiling milk into mixture in thin stream. Pour into pan, and set on low heat stirring constantly until thickened enough to coat spoon.

Remove from heat and add orange and gelatin mixture. Beat for a moment. Place in clean mixing bowl. Beat 5 egg whites until soft peaks form. Gradually add sugar, beating constantly until stiff peaks form. With rubber spatuala fold egg whites into hot custard. Place in refrigerator. Fold several times while cooling.

When cool, but not set, fold in whipping cream which has been beaten until it forms ribbons. Place in graham cracker pie crust and put in freezer. Let freeze 6 hours. Serve topped with whipped cream and fresh Florida orange slices.

Serves: 6-8

ORANGE 'n APPLE PIE

5	medium size Florida oranges
5	medium size apples
3/4	cup light brown sugar
3/4	tablespoon cornstarch
1/4	teaspoon salt
1/4	teaspoon cinnamon
1	tablespoon grated Florida orange rind
20	ounces cake flour
1	teaspoon baking powder
2	eggs
4	ounces butter
4	ounces Crisco shortening

Peel and section the oranges. Peel and quarter and slice the apples. Mix well light brown sugar, salt, cornstarch and orange gratings. Next, combine with orange sections and sliced apples.

Prepare pie crust, using flour, baking powder, butter and Crisco shortening. Instead of water use eggs.

Use half of pie crust for the bottom part. Pour mixture in pie pan, covering with remainder of dough. Brush top with melted butter and sprinkle with sugar. Bake at 375° F. for 40 minutes. Serve at room temperature.

Serves: 6-10

PINK SUNSET PARFAIT PIE

1	tablespoon unflavored gelatin
1/2	cup Florida orange juice
1	pint vanilla ice cream, melted
2	egg whites
1/4	cup granulated sugar
6	Florida orange sections, coarsely chopped
1	9-inch baked pastry shell
2	cups whipped cream, sweetened

In a saucepan, mix gelatin and orange juice. Let stand several minutes. Stir over low heat; stir in ice cream. Chill, stirring occasionally, until mixture mounds slightly when dropped from a spoon. In large mixing bowl, beat egg whites until soft peaks form; gradually add sugar and beat until stiff. Fold into gelatin mixture. Fold in orange sections. Pour into prepared crust. Chill until firm. Garnish with whipped cream and additional orange sections.

Serves: 6-8

ORANGE AND ALMOND CAKE WITH

1	cup blanched almonds
1	cup granulated sugar
1/2	pound unsalted butter at room temperature
1	tablespoon grated orange rind
4	eggs
1 1/4	cups all purpose flour
1	teaspoon double acting baking powder
1/4	teaspoon salt
1/3	cup Florida orange juice
1/2	teaspoon vanilla
	Glaze (recipe follows)

Preheat oven to 350⁰ F. Butter well a springform pan and sprinkle with flour. Invert pan over sink to shake out excess flour. In a blender or food processor, grind the almonds very fine. Add sugar and process until well-blended. Cream the butter by using an electric beater until fluffy. Add the almond mixture and beat until blended. Add the grated orange rind and eggs one at a time, beating well after each addition. Sift together flour, baking powder and salt. Add this mixture to the butter mixture alternating with the orange juice - beginning and ending with flour mixture. Mix lightly after each addition.

Pour batter into 9" springform pan and bake in the oven for 50-55 minutes or until an inserted toothpick comes out clean. Let cake cool in the pan for about 10 minutes. Unmold cake onto a cake rack and let it cool completely.

This cake may be served plain or glazed. It may be refrigerated for 2-3 days.

Makes: 1 9-inch cake

ORANGE GLAZE

Glaze

1/2	cup Florida orange juice
1/2	teaspoon grated orange rind
2 1/2	cups powdered sugar
	Candied orange peel for garnish or strips of orange peel

Pour Florida orange juice into a bowl and add orange rind and sugar. Whisk until smooth and thick. Pour the glaze over the cake, letting it drip down the sides. Let stand for about an hour until the glaze hardens. Decorate with candied orange peel or with fresh orange peel strips.

Serves: 8-10

FLORIDA ORANGE PANCAKES

2	egg yolks
1/2	teaspoon salt
1/2	teaspoon baking powder
2	tablespoons Florida honey
2	cups Florida orange sections, chopped fine
1	cup sifted flour
2	egg whites, stiffly beaten
	Butter and oil for frying.

Beat the yolks, salt and honey together, stir in orange sections and flour and fold in beaten egg whites. Heat butter and oil to cover bottom of skillet, about 1/4 inch. Drop batter by tablespoon. Brown on both sides. Serve hot. Garnish with sour cream and jelly.

Serves: 4

QUICK AND LUSCIOUS
ORANGE BREAD

1 1/2	cups all purpose flour
1	teaspoon double acting baking powder
1/4	teaspoon salt
2/3	cup sugar
	Grated rind of 1 Florida orange
2	eggs, beaten
1/2	cup fresh Florida orange juice (About 2 oranges squeezed)
1/4	cup shortening, melted
3	tablespoons orange marmalade

Preheat oven to 375⁰ F. Butter a loaf pan well. Set aside.

In a bowl, sift together flour, baking powder, salt and sugar. Add the orange rind and mix well. In another bowl, lightly whisk together eggs, orange juice and shortening. Stir wet ingredients into the flour mixture until just moistened. Spoon into the prepared loaf pan carefully. Spread the orange marmalade on top of the batter, and bake in a preheated oven for 30-35 minutes or until an inserted toothpick comes out clean.

Cool for about 10 minutes, then turn out and cool completely on a cake rack. If desired, spread more orange marmalade over the bread.

Yield: 1 loaf

MAMA'S ORANGE BISCUITS

2 1/2	cups all-purpose flour
3	teaspoons baking powder
1	teaspoon salt
2	tablespoons grated Florida orange rind
1/2	cup shortening
3/4	cup milk (more or less)
18	sugar cubes
1	cup Florida orange juice

Preheat oven to 425⁰ F. Sift flour, baking powder and salt into a bowl. Add orange rind. Add shortening and cut in with pastry blender or a knife until the mixture resembles a coarse meal. Use just enough milk to form a dough that is soft but not sticky. Blend mixture gently with a fork. Turn out on a floured board and knead for about 30 seconds or until smooth.

Roll the dough out to 1/2-inch thickness and cut with a floured biscuit cutter. Place on an ungreased baking sheet. Dip sugar cubes individually into the orange juice and place a dipped cube In top of each biscuit. Bake in the preheated oven for about 12 minutes or until golden brown. Serve hot. The biscuits may be refrigerated and reheated in regular oven or microwave.

Yield: 18 biscuits

HOW TO PEEL AND SECTION FLORIDA ORANGES

Chill oranges before preparing. To section the fruit:

1. Cut slice from top, then cut off peel in strips from top to bottom, cutting deeply enough to remove white membrane. Then cut slice from bottom.
2. OR, cut off peel round and round, spiral fashion. Go over fruit again, removing any white membrane.
3. Cut alongside each dividing membrane from outside to the middle of core.
4. Remove section by section over bowl to retain juice from fruit.

ORANGES: EARLY AND LATE SEASON

VALENCIA ORANGE Medium to large size, round to oval shape, yellow to orange color (sometimes tinged with green) with a smooth, thin peel. Usually seedless or with only a few seeds. Valencias have orange colored flesh, which is loaded with golden juice of fine rich flavor and aroma.

PARSON BROWN ORANGE Medium to large size, round, light orange color with pebbly peel, often tinged with green. Usually a few seeds. Deep golden juice, rich flavor.

PINEAPPLE ORANGE Medium to large size, round to oval, orange color, pebbly peel. Has some seeds. The pineapple orange is acclaimed for its juicy sweetness.

HAMLIN ORANGE Medium size, round to oval, deep yellow to orange color with a smooth, thin peel. Usually seedless. An excellent juice orange.

NAVEL ORANGE Large to extra large fruit, round to oval, deep yellow to orange color. Pebbly, medium thick peel. Usually seedless. Peels and sections very easily.

re-order information

Copy this form and send to:

P.O. Box 14441
St. Petersburg, Florida 33733-4441

Please send me _____ copies of **Famous Florida!**[®] Recipes from the Orange Grove at $5.95 per copy. Add $2.50 for postage and handling for the first book ordered and .50 for each additional copy. Make check payable to *Seaside Publishing*

Name _____

Street _____

City _____

State & Zip _____

re-order information

Copy this form and send to:

Seaside
Publishing, Inc.
P.O. Box 14441
St. Petersburg, Florida 33733-4441

Please send me _____ copies of **Famous Florida!**® Recipes from **the Orange Grove** at $5.95 per copy. Add $2.50 for postage and handling for the first book ordered and .50 for each additional copy. Make check payable to *Seaside Publishing*

Name _____

Street _____

City _____

State & Zip _____

ABOUT THE AUTHOR:

Joyce LaFray, acknowledged to be one of Florida's foremost food experts, has earned plaudits for her ability to educate and entertain in a cornucopia of media settings.

Food critic, author, lecturer, editor and spokesperson for many of Florida's leading corporations and foodstuffs, Joyce has developed a rapidly growing, enthusiastic group of fans.

Because of her recognized status as a culinary expert, Joyce has been called on by many of the nation's leading food writers to borrow her expertise and intimate knowledge of the Florida and Carribean scene.

http:\\www.famous florida.com

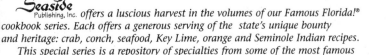

Seaside Publishing, Inc. *offers a luscious harvest in the volumes of our Famous Florida!® cookbook series. Each offers a generous serving of the state's unique bounty and heritage: crab, conch, seafood, Key Lime, orange and Seminole Indian recipes.*

This special series is a repository of specialties from some of the most famous restaurants in Florida. Many of the recipes are found nowhere else; all recipes are delicious! Joyce LaFray, acknowledged to be one of Florida's foremost food experts, has earned plaudits for her ability to educate, entertain and critique.

Enjoy this very special tour of Famous Florida!®